RADICAL REVERENCE for YOUR Life ...

How I learned to Live with More Joy and Wonder

DANNY BADER

Published by Desert Soul Publishing.

www.dannybader.com

Edited by Sue Reynard

Book cover design by Christy Collins, Constellation Book Services.

Printed in the United States of America.

ISBN 13 TP: 978-1-7327066-7-5

ISBN 13 Ebook: 978-1-7327066-8-2

arrfY1 ™ is a trademark of Danny Bader

Dedication

To my family and friends, whose love and presence make every day brighter, deeper, and more meaningful.

To those who choose to honor this life, embracing the extraordinary within the ordinary.

And to those who feel lost, weary, or uncertain—this is for you. May you find strength in the pages ahead, knowing that within you lies a powerful Light, waiting to be rekindled.

 I chose the sunflower for the cover of this book because it's my favorite flower. Its ability to turn toward the sun symbolizes the human journey toward enlightenment and self-realization.

So for those who seek meaning, purpose, and connection with Spirit, let the sunflowers in this book be a reminder to always cultivate **arrfYl**, a radical reverence for YOUR life.

Peace.

Danny

Table of Contents

Preface: Making Reverence Radical. vii

#1: BE MORE SPIRIT. 1

#2: LIVE YOUR TRUTH 19

#3: LOVE YOUR PEOPLE FIERCELY . . . and LET THEM
LOVE YOU. 33

#4: TRUST YOU ARE A RESILIENT HUMAN BEING. 49

#5: EMBRACE THE STRUGGLE. 59

#6: ALWAYS ~~TRY~~ WORK TO BE BETTER. 77

#7: CONTEMPLATE YOUR MORTALITY. 95

Epilogue 103

About the Author. 104

Preface

Making Reverence Radical

Living with a radical reverence for YOUR life means recognizing that the approximately 23,000 breaths you take and the 100,000 heartbeats you experience each day are not guaranteed—and it's up to you to make each and every one of those breaths count.

Now, I know that the cynic in each of you might be thinking: "Great, this guy has me pondering my mortality. I'm so inspired right now I might not even need to read further." Yes, I get it. But stick with me.

Reverence, to me, means humbling oneself in recognition of something greater—what I call "greater than self" or God. You may have another name for this, whether it's Source, Universe, or Consciousness, and that's perfectly fine.

I believe most people live with what I think of now as a "regular" reverence for life. They hold human life as sacred, and honor the inherent value of each human being. This regular reverence forms a kind of white noise in the background of their lives—something they take for granted and don't consciously think about every day. It's an attitude often leads us to get caught up in the bullshit and trivialities of life.

That's why I use the term "radical" to indicate that I want us to go beyond what is usual. Together, the combined term "radical reverence" means understanding that fulfillment and resilience are more about consciously connecting to something "greater than self." It means challenging yourself to think consciously—every day—about how you're living your life and how you're treating those around you.

When I talk about a radical reverence for life, I'm always challenged with this question: "Danny, do you truly live with a radical reverence for your life, or do you just say you do?" I love getting that question because it has a way of unsettling me, pushing me to think deeply—and, in my case, sometimes kicking my ass.

My own attempts to live with radical reverence wasn't a simple or easy path. It began more than 30 years ago after a tragic electrocution accident where both a friend and I were struck by around 8,000 volts, resulting in both our deaths. Fortunately for me, I came back to life. My friend didn't. It seemed like such a random event, with no purpose or cause, no logic as to why I survived and my friend didn't that I've often struggled to live with a radical reverence for my own life. Spoiler alert: I wasn't always successful.

But now, having reached 60 and having lost too many loved ones, I am more committed than ever to embracing this way of life. And it's got me thinking about how I can help people like you live with a radical reference for YOUR life, a concept I abbreviate as **arrfYl,** pronounced "r-fill."

In my own journey of personal growth, I've met with some remarkable people, like a young man with a terminal illness who taught me about loving your people fiercely. I've read and researched widely, using sources ranging from science to professional athletes and Antarctic explorers. Along the way, I discovered seven timeless principles—not invented by me—that exemplify what it takes to live a more reverent and positive life. They are:

1 -- Be more Spirit

2 -- Live your Truth

3 -- Love your people fiercely

4 -- Trust you are a resilient human being

5 -- Embrace the struggle

6 -- Always ~~try~~ work to be better

7 -- Contemplate your mortality

I've seen people who practice these seven principles and embody this radical reverence for life, and they are joyful, observant, thankful, fulfilled, trusting, and resilient. Conversely, those who lack it often seem frustrated, impatient, stuck in the past or future, aloof, mean-spirited, selfish, full of blame and regret, and overwhelmed by negative energies. I've been there, too. So, where are you right now? Do you live with **arrfYl**?

I've also seen many people (including myself, at times) for whom **arrfYl** is fleeting. We embrace all or most of these concepts during tragic events like 9/11, mass shootings, the COVID-19 pandemic, or after attending a funeral for someone young. But then, a few days later, "real life" intervened and we return to the numb routine of phones, social media, TV, traffic jams, inboxes, negative news, and endless to-do lists.

What I want you to do right now is imagine holding onto a perpetual mindset of radical reverence for the breaths you take and the beats of your heart, recognizing them as gifts rather than guarantees. Imagine practicing these principles every day—or at least much more often than you do now. How would this change your thoughts, actions, relationships, health, career, spirituality, fulfillment, and resilience?

This book explores these concepts, and I encourage you to reflect on them and experiment with them in your own life. Deal? An incredible side benefit is that when you live with **arrfYl** and hold a radical reverence for YOUR life, you naturally extend this reverence, this much-needed respect, to others.

Here's a powerful question for you: If you were conscious when you were about to draw your last breath, and you knew it—would you smile? Someone who lived with a radical reverence for their life would.

#1

BE MORE SPIRIT

The human spirit is more powerful than any drug, and it needs to be nourished with work, play, friendship, and family. These are the things that matter.[1]

—Robin Williams

---

1 https://www.azquotes.com/quote/576253?ref=human-spirit

Be More Spirit

Read again the quote on the previous page from Robin Williams about the power of the human spirit. Perhaps even read it aloud. Do you agree with it? I do. I admire the work, insight, and brilliance of Robin Williams, and like many, I was sad when he passed. I believe it's possible his life could have been extended had he connected more with his own Spirit, for it is the strength of the Spirit that defeats our demons.

I like the definition of Spirit as *the nonphysical part of a person, which is the seat of emotions and character—the soul.* You have this nonphysical source of inner wisdom, guidance, and love. You don't connect *to* your Spirit; it's not some external energy source. You connect *with* your Spirit, building a bridge to something that's already a part of you.

Sometimes in life, we are too much human and not enough Spirit. Have you moved through a struggle in life and experienced the resilience of your Spirit? If you're like most of us, you're nodding your head and recalling a time in your life when you hit the proverbial rock bottom and had only one choice: either let life win, let life beat you *or* tap into the power of your Spirit and move through your struggle. Trust me, I know you are not here to let life win . . . it's the other way around.

If you find yourself in a challenging period of your life as you read this, I want you to remember that deep down—in your Spirit—you possess the strength to emerge on the other side. Keep pushing forward. Keep moving. Those who have faced adversity understand the significance of their Spirit, especially during the most trying times. Your Spirit desires only what is best for you; it cannot create pain and despair.

My Spirit Lived When I Died

For those of you who aren't familiar with my own personal history, when I was almost 29, I worked as a roofer for two great brothers—Bruce and Stew—who owned a small roofing company. One day, Bruce and I lowered a metal ladder at the end of a workday. He was ready to go home and take his young son fishing. I was prepared to tell my girlfriend—now my wonderful wife of 30+ years—that I was moving back to Aspen, CO, to get my real estate license, sell lots of expensive homes, make lots of money, and ski a lot. This plan changed in an instant.

Bruce and I lowered the ladder, which struck a high-voltage electric line we thought we were clear of. Afterward, investigators of the accident said we only hit it by 2-3 inches at the top of the ladder, a slight margin of error and a tragic margin. Approximately 8,000 volts came down the ladder and into me and Bruce. We both died. According to Stew, who attempted CPR on me and stopped as it wasn't working, I was dead for six or seven minutes. Only I came back to life. The electricity entered my hands and exited my feet, socks, and boots. Four holes in my feet, one on each side of each foot. (See photo, next page.)

When my body died that day of the accident, there was an energy that did not. I was conscious, just not in the worldly way we all know. It was different. I was aware I was dying . . . or dead. There was no fear or pain, just *peace* but that word only scratches the surface of what I felt and experienced. It was not of this world as I had come to know it. I remember seeing my buddy coming down the ladder, and I was yelling at him to go to his brother; I was not calling for help for me. This is the last thing I remember of this world.

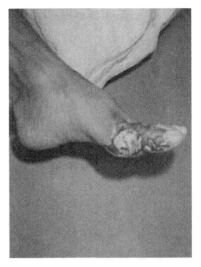

Danny's left foot 10 days after the accident.

After I came back to life and he and I talked at the accident scene, I told him I'd seen him coming down the ladder and was yelling at him to get to his brother. What he said confirmed my death for me. He shook his head and said, "You didn't say anything." He came to me first. My eyes were rolled back in my head, and foam covered my lips as he delivered CPR for a few minutes. He gave me up for dead, ran across the street to call 911, and ran back past me—still dead—to go to his brother.

In my first book, *Back to Life, The Path of Resilience,* you can read about this part of my journey. It's the story of a young man named Jake, who has an accident like mine. This accident was what screenwriters call the inciting incident . . . you know, the thing that happens to the main character in a movie, and afterward, their life will never be the same. Dying . . . and then coming back to life was my inciting incident.

For about ten days or so before my accident, I had not been talking to my mom. I was living at home, and we'd argued about me, how I was living my life, and how I was non-committal to my girlfriend, Lisa (my wonderful wife now of 30+ years). I was angry and defensive, probably because deep down, I knew Mom was right. I see now that my connection with my Spirit was weak. I immaturely chose to ignore her until the Monday night before the Tuesday accident. I had not seen her in a few days as I'd been out late and came home when she was in bed and then was up and out in the morning before she awoke. For a reason I did not know then and realized was the influence of my Spirit, I came home, walked into the room where my mom was watching TV, and kissed her good night. No conversation, no apology. I just kissed her. The next time we saw one another was in the hospital after the accident the next day. First, she asked me, "Why did you kiss me last night?" I had no answer then, I do now . . . Spirit.

And then the next day, less than 24 hours later, not only did the 8,000 or so volts explode out of both sides of both feet . . . it also did more damage. It severed my connection with my Spirit. I know this now. I did not know it then. This lost connection to my Spirit led me down the dark path of pain, despair, regret, and a bunch of other negative emotions, feelings, and mindsets.

I've come to understand that the most basic need is for you to connect with your Spirit, the divine essence within.

A New Foundation for the Hierarchy of Needs

Do you recall Abraham Maslow's (1908-1970) Hierarchy of Needs? I was first introduced to this pyramid model in the mid-1970s.

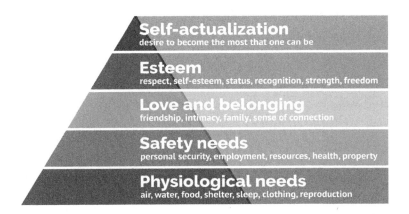

Maslow's Hierarchy of Needs

Dr. Maslow's psychological theory suggests that there are layers to our motivations as shown in the image above. When I Googled Maslow's Hierarchy of Needs, I came across this explanation for his theory at medicalnewstoday.com:

> *The lowest and biggest levels represent the basic and highest priority needs that are essential for survival.*

> *The smaller and higher sections represent self-esteem and self-actualization, which are essential for fulfillment or emotional well-being.*

The lowest level, represents our most fundamental need essential for survival: food, shelter, etc. (what Maslow calls "physiological needs"). Only once those needs are met can we pay attention to the next layer up ("safety needs") and so on up the pyramid. Our quest for fulfillment, change, and personal growth is at the top of the pyramid, indicating that in Maslow's mind, we can pay attention to it only after we've addressed everything below it.

I understand what Maslow offers us in this model. He believes our actions are motivated by specific physiological and psychological needs that progress from basic to complex. The model can support your quest for more robust mental health and overall wellness, by making it clear that you won't be able to pay proper attention to those needs unless you've addressed the wider, more basic levels first.

The mental health and wellness of people has become—and rightfully so—a significant focus for leaders within organizations. While Maslow suggests we pursue all these needs, they may not be in the order Maslow laid out. Maslow would likely agree that **arrfYl** is obtained as one moves up the pyramid.

This pyramid made sense to me when I first learned about it. You can see it evident in everyday life when people say things like:

- "I'm so hungry . . . I could eat a horse."

- "I'm freezing . . . I need to get warm.'

- "I'm exhausted . . . I need a good night's sleep."

- "I'm so horny . . . _____. (I'll let you fill in the blank on this one.)

These are all needs at the bottom of the pyramid that people need to address before they can deal with anything else in their lives.

However, as I approach my 60s, I feel there's more nuance and even conflict in what motivates people. I've seen people who are not so interested in the lower levels. Have you ever seen a teenager in love for the first time? They are "so in love" that they often disregard food and safety. Have you ever been so focused on a project or the creation of something that someone asks, "Have you eaten?" and you reply, "No, I guess I forgot."

I've also seen people addicted to self-actualization and growth—sometimes referred to as "self-help junkies"—who neglect the security (financial) and employment needs, and perhaps even the Love and belonging needs, and go to endless personal growth seminars and spiritual retreats in pursuit of Maslow's top of the pyramid—Self-actualization. The point I make is that each need is unique to the person pursuing it, and this pursuit is dynamic.

Now I realize I should not be messing around with Maslow's model; he was a brilliant dude, so if you see him, please don't tell him (ha-ha). I hear him now, "And you tell that Danny Bader guy to stop messing with my model." I appreciate Maslow's work and his passion for supporting us on our journey; I just felt his model—based on my life experience to this point—needed another layer, a steadfast base level of the pyramid. As the model suggests, this new layer will serve as the foundation for the other needs. I call this new level *Connect with your Spirit* (see figure, next page).

Self-actualization
desire to become the most that one can be

Esteem
respect, self-esteem, status, recognition, strength, freedom

Love and belonging
friendship, intimacy, family, sense of connection

Safety needs
personal security, employment, resources, health, property

Physiological needs
air, water, food, shelter, sleep, clothing, reproduction

Connect with Your Spirit

My version of Maslow's hierarchy, adding Spirit as the foundation

Feel Your Spirit

I'm one of eight children; my sister, Trish, is the oldest, and then seven boys. Trish was married to a wonderful man, Bobby, who became one of my best friends. He passed away in May of 2022 from ALS. I had canceled a speaking event and hurried back home from California when he took his final turn toward death. I was in the hospital room with Trish and my nephews and niece when Bobby passed. He took his last breath, and a moment later, as we all cried and talked out loud to Bobby, my sister looked at me across the bed and said, "D, did you feel that?" I nodded, smiling as tears rolled down my face. I had what some of you may call goose bumps when your arms and the back of your neck tingle and you shake a bit. I call them "Spirit shivers," I'm thankful each time I get them when the Spirit of a deceased loved one "shows up" to let me know they're okay. Yes, I had felt Bobby's Spirit leave. I bet you've also felt the Spirit of one of your deceased people, and it's a good thing.

The Human Spirit has never been attributed or responsible for anything bad or negative. Instead, it's referenced as the source of courage, resilience, persistence, creativity, forgiveness, empathy, love, and Faith when "all is lost." This is what I mean when I say in the title of this chapter . . . be more Spirit. Our lives are better when we connect with the Spirit. We create lives of fulfillment and resilience, move away from the pain of your past, and are not stuck in the fabricated fear of our futures. You are here, focused, holding a radical reverence for YOUR life.

When you get a chance, be sure to Google "the man in the red bandana," you'll be inspired by the story of 24-year-old Welles Crowther, who I'm confident was strongly connected with his Spirit on the fateful day of 9/11 in New York City. When he was six years old, his father gave him a red bandana, which became his trademark, and he wore it under all his sports uniforms in high school and as a lacrosse player at Boston College. At the time of the attack on the World Trade Center, Crowther was an equities trader working on the 104th floor of the South Tower and a volunteer firefighter.

Eyewitnesses that day reported a man with a red bandana over his mouth and nose who appeared out of nowhere, spoke calmly and is said to have been responsible for going back into the South Tower several times, carrying one woman down on his back, and saving at least eighteen people.

Welles Crowther's body was found six months later. When asked about Welles' name etched into the wall of the 911 Memorial, his mother, Alison, said, "To me, it's a perfect representation of his Spirit, and it's very soothing."

Tragedy and struggle are the backdrop for many stories that show the power of the human Spirit. You must not wait for tragedy or struggle; you must connect with your Spirit daily, regardless of what's happening in your life. We grow out of two forces: curiosity and tragedy. Don't wait for tragedy to come; be curious each day about connecting with your Spirit.

When you get caught up in the daily grind of life and begin to go through the motions week after week, you are being too human and not enough Spirit. Work to reverse this and be "too much Spirit," which is impossible; one cannot have too much Spirit.

If you're a Christian or have at least heard of the historical figure Jesus Christ, you may find his last words interesting.

It is recorded that Jesus died on the cross during his crucifixion; his last words were, "Father, into your hands, I commend my Spirit." Regardless of your beliefs about who Jesus of Nazareth was, you see here another case supporting my understanding of the Spirit as our 4th energy. I believe Jesus was who he claimed to be. I always enjoy seeing a dove—the Christian symbol for Spirit—in images or within the beautiful stained-glass windows of many churches. Jesus' body hung on the cross, broken and battered and punctured, and while his heart, brain, and lungs were weak, it was the departure of His Spirit that caused His body to cease working when He offered it up.

Ego Is the Opposite of Spirit

I believe the opposite of Spirit is ego, one's sense of self-worth, or the perception one has about oneself and one's identity in this world. It may also be called self-esteem, self-confidence, self-respect, or self-image. For me, it's how one sees oneself in this world. It's how one engages with life, their job, their relationships, their commitment to growth, and their treatment of others. It encompasses one's thoughts, beliefs, and values. It is being human.

When you are born, I believe your Spirit is strong, and then the world goes to work, adding layers to your connection with your Spirit. Your connection to ego—not good or bad—is your focus on being *in* this world as a human being. It causes you to react to the ongoings of this world and focus on being the individual you are. It's the place where all our human emotions are available to us. Some of these are labeled as bad—anger, guilt, regret, blame, judgment, etc. The ego is where comparison to others and competition and the will to be "better, wealthier, more attractive, more admired" than others reside.

When you are born, your Spirit is strong, and then the world goes to work, adding layers to your connection with your Spirit.

I've read that the Spirit is referred to as the true self and the ego as the false self. I understand this means putting yourself first when operating from EGO. When you're connected with your Spirit, you put others first and continually grow into someone who brings love, peace, joy, and resilience to the world . . . which is what I believe we are all ultimately here for.

The ego is responsible for **what** you create during your lifetime . . . the Spirit is responsible for the **how**. Engaging in this world from your point of ego is not wrong or bad; you need both. Achieving wealth and nice material possessions is not wrong or bad. Competition to do a great job, continue using your talents, and grow in wisdom is a noble pursuit . . . what's essential to consider is how you achieve these. Does greed drive the person? Do they lose focus on their family to pursue material success? Do they sacrifice some of their excellent values to achieve? Do they forget their human obligation to be a person of good morals?

The definition I use for ego is "**e**nergy **g**one **o**bnoxious." When we become guided by our ego, with the Spirit in the background, we become obnoxious. Remember my enhancement to Maslow's model?

Over the past few years, I've read some of Ryan Holiday's books and followed him on social media. Ryan is the founder of the website dailystoic.com, and one of the books I read is *Ego Is The Enemy*, which I often recommend. He once said, "Do you act for your strong moral code? Goodness—the highest good for the most number of people?"

In his YouTube video also titled *Ego is the Enemy* (less than 5 minutes), Ryan says: "The enemy is inside of you, it's your ego. The ego is the enemy because it prevents us from learning, holds us back, and makes us overreach. The essence of this book is how to battle with that inner force. It's the thing that destroys empires and great companies and brilliant artists and tears apart relationships and partnerships and all that stuff." He then says, "Confidence is the opposite of ego. Based on real skills and real self-awareness," this is what I've come to describe as a "healthy ego." It means someone is operating in the world knowing they can continue growing and serving others until their last day.

Be a person with a healthy ego that operates with your Spirit at the core. When approaching life from this perspective, you'll have a strong sense of self-worth, exude confidence instead of arrogance, and seek to build healthy, respectful relationships that lift others up and encourage them. You will quite simply continue to grow into your goodness.

Building Your Own Foundation

I believe we're always acting out of ego; it's our path to the world and daily engagement with life. It's just that I've come to understand life is better when Spirit is the foundation.

I recall when I traveled to the Outer Banks of North Carolina several months after my accident so many years ago. It was the off-season for this beach community. I went there as depressed and full of desperate despair as possible. I had no connection with my Spirit . . . until the stillness of this quiet beach town allowed me to hear something—not with my ears—it was more profound; it was a hearing within my Spirit. It led me to go home, get better, and trust it will all be okay.

I've come to understand your Spirit resides in stillness. It does not come through your social media accounts, Netflix, to-do list, or inbox. I know this voice saved my life, and I believe it was the voice I heard deep in my Soul that the Sufi poet Rumi references in one of my favorite quotes:

"There's a voice that doesn't use words. Listen."

Your Spirit must be the foundation for your engagement in the world. You must let the fruits of the Spirit, such as love, joy, peace, patience, kindness, goodness, faithfulness, gentleness, and self-control, lead you. I've presided at some weddings for young couples and always give them a piece of wall art listing these fruits of the Spirit. I encourage them to hang it somewhere prominent and focus on creating these in their relationship and home.

Please don't take this as preaching. Only you can determine whether you are living with too much human (ego) or are leading by Spirit. You've seen the fantastic accomplishments of people grounded in Spirit: Mother Teresa, Gandhi, Nelson Mandela, and countless others whose names we will never know. Mother Teresa captures the power of leading from the Spirit when she says,

"Be kind and merciful. Let no one ever come to you without coming away better and happier."

Connection with Your Spirit, your Soul, is a tremendous source and foundation for living with a radical reverence for YOUR life. Einstein referenced this when he said, "The Soul given to each of us is moved by the same living Spirit that moves the Universe." Right on, Albert. Well said.

Your Spirit does not need to wrestle with your ego . . . your humanity. It is not its job. You need both. Neither needs to "win."

Your Spirit is here to dance with your humanity, and you must walk onto life's dance floor each morning you come back to life, hold out your hand, and invite your Spirit to dance as you head out into your days, weeks, months, years . . . YOUR LIFE. Then, allow your Spirit to guide your dance moves as you fulfill your human dreams, responsibilities, and roles.

The English philosopher Bernard Williams said it best: "Man never made any material as resilient as the human spirit."

Be more Spirit.

#2

LIVE YOUR TRUTH

"Truth is like the sun. You can shut it out for a time, but it ain't going away."

—Elvis Presley, "The King"

Live Your Truth

I've become used to hearing the term "live your truth" from my oldest child, Luke. It's a mantra for him. He lives *his* truth as a gay 30-something man and encourages others to live *theirs*. He's inspired me to hold up a mirror and look at the life I have created and continue to develop for myself. I'm happy to report that his coaching has encouraged me to grow. When one "holds up the mirror," so to speak, they're stepping boldly into their vulnerability, seeing their truth, and making changes where needed. When you have the focus and courage to make this self-reflection a habit, you will likely experience some external resistance, perhaps internal as well.

Truth is defined as *that which is true or in accordance with fact or reality.* The fact and the reality are you were born YOU, a unique person intended to create and live out YOUR reality. We all know deep inside what this is and how we should live it. Sometimes, your truth lies at the surface early in life, and sometimes, not. Either way, it is there, and you will experience more joy when you live it. It comes down to being yourself in a world that promotes conformity and imitation—trying to make you like everyone else. (Have you ever seen or felt this through social media?)

We all know deep inside what our truth is and how we should live it. Sometimes, our truth lies at the surface early in life, and sometimes not.

Luke's coming out as a gay young man was a difficult part of his life's journey, and the love, pride, and respect I had for him have been enhanced and multiplied as I've observed and supported him. His Catholic family surrounded Luke, and there was the fear of rejection, although thankfully, none of this happened. There were, however, perspectives and conversations of "not understanding" and ignorant opinions that this was Luke's "choice." You do not have to understand the "truth" that someone else lives; you just need to love them.

Luke offered me an incredible eye-opener to this when one day I said to him. "Luke, I love you and always will. You just love differently than me." Luke took a deep breath of patience toward his well-meaning "old man" and responded, "Dad. I don't love any differently. Love is love." It was my turn to take a deep breath, slowly and silently processing what he said, then responded with a hug and, "Thanks, Luke, I got it." You see, I was thinking of the physical expression of love. A definition of love I like is *a set of emotions and behaviors characterized by intimacy, passion, and commitment.* Love is much, much more than physical. In all the ways that matter, Luke's love is the same as mine or yours or anyone else's.

Conforming to Ourselves, Not to Others

I've come to understand the world wants us to conform to many rules, stereotypes, and popular ways of living, while our Spirit (remember that?) wants us to grow and flourish into the person we indeed are.

There likely have been times when you've conformed for one reason or another and made a choice not connected with your values. I did so when I was 18 when I chose accounting as my major when I headed into college. (No offense to you fantastic accountants out there. My friend, Scott, is an excellent accountant, and I value his insight and guidance.)

Why did I choose accounting? My mom had asked what I would major in as I entered college, and I responded, "I think I'll go in undeclared." She smiled, shaking her head, and said, "I think not." She said I should major in accounting as it would give me a solid understanding of business. Deep down, I did not want to be an accountant. I knew deep inside that being an accountant would not be living my truth. So I resisted and asked her to give me one good reason. She replied she would give me two: First, she mentioned that I got good grades in high school accounting. I disputed that it was basic accounting and easy. Second, she told me of a friend of my older sister who'd just graduated with an accounting degree, had gotten a great job, and had just bought a brand-new Honda Accord. So, I surrendered, fully accepting my defeat, only to realize years later I had made a significant life decision based on what Japanese imported car I could afford upon graduation.

I never formally practiced a day of Accounting and realized the pain, struggle, and misdirected focus that comes when you're not living your truth.

Find Your Focus

Let me offer you some insight from Laird Small, a guy who teaches golf at the Pebble Beach Golf Academy. I read an article once where Small explained a technique he used with students. He calls it NATO, an acronym standing for *not attached to outcome* (not the North Atlantic Treaty Organization!). The point is that when his students hit a lousy shot, their focus—defined as your concentration of attention & energy—would almost automatically go to how the poor shot affected the outcome they wanted, which could be making par on the hole or breaking 80, 90, or 100 for their round. NATO would suggest that golfers focus more on being outdoors with their friends, enjoying the beautiful scenery and being thankful for their health. That is, they will be happier overall if they focus on things other than the scorecard.

In life, your focus is your most significant and most valuable commodity. Let me repeat: YOUR FOCUS IS YOUR MOST SIGNIFICANT AND MOST VALUABLE COMMODITY. Most people talk about time management, while I talk about focus management. You cannot control time. You *can* control your focus; your power comes from focusing on what you can control.

Your focus in your most significant and most valuable commodity.

Small would coach his students that the goal of making par on the hole or shooting a specific score is good and should be considered. Then, he would ask them what they could control right now. Sometimes, they'd get the answer right; other times, he'd have to tell them, "Right now, you can only control the next shot." You see, all they had right then was their next shot; they could not get back the ones they'd already hit, and they could not play the rest of their shots . . . just the next shot. If they could consistently focus and execute well enough on each "next shot," they would likely achieve their goal.

It's the same with living your truth. When you know your values and live them each day, make them the basis for your "next shot" over and over again . . . you will likely achieve your goals, turn your visions into reality, and live with a radical reverence for YOUR life.

Truth <==> Purpose

How do you live your truth? Yes, great question. Let's take this from concept to reality. Living your values puts you on your path of purpose—living your truth. You don't need to *find* your purpose; I don't believe it's lost. When someone asks me, "Danny, can you help me find my purpose?" I respond, "No." They usually look at me with some surprise as I continue, "You don't need to find your purpose. It ain't lost. You just need to design your outer life around your inner values."

I believe living your values and the beliefs you hold is the foundation for living with purpose. Purpose is the reason for which something is done or created or for which something exists. Your purpose is to know your values and live them through your actions each day, always doing your best to grow more vital in living them . . . and supporting others to do the same. You were created to do this.

Now I realize some of you are saying, "I see Danny, but what about when I get off course, distracted, and move away from living my values? What do I do then?" Great question and I believe St. Francis states it simply when he reminds that each day is the opportunity to begin again. If you're living your values and your truth . . . great. If not, begin right now moving back to this.

St. Francis DeSales wrote:

"It is right that you should begin again every day. There is no better way to complete the spiritual life than to be ever beginning it over again."

He encouraged himself—and us—to know that each day we come back to life is a precious opportunity to connect with our Spirit and have that as the foundation for all we focus on achieving in life . . . materially and spiritually. Knowing your values and living your truth comes from your inner wisdom; it's just a "knowing," sometimes supported by the logic of this world, other times not.

If you've never read the book *The Top Five Regrets of the Dying* by Bronnie Ware, I suggest you do. The book is based on Ware's experience with people at the end of their life. The first regret is *I wish I'd had the courage to live a life true to myself, not the life others expected of me.* This is validation of the need for you to live your truth. Ware tells of Grace, a sweet woman in her 80s with a terminal illness. One quote that hit me was when Grace told Bronnie, "It's not like I wanted a grand life. I am a good person and didn't wish to harm anyone. But I wanted to do things for me, too, and I just didn't have the courage."

Imagine you're nearing the end of your life and looking back to see what you would have done differently. The main thing is that you would have lived a more authentic life designed around YOUR values and interests, not those others expected you to live. You can avoid a lot of potential sadness and misery by paying attention to this top regret of dying people and making sure it will not be yours. Do you need to create some courage to do things for you?

When you live your truth, you do not judge others, do not need validation from them, and do not take things personally. When you live your truth, you are not swayed by the opinion of others. And you don't need to "win" as the world defines it— the material success of money, houses, cars, vacations, etc. Those things are not intrinsically good or bad; you must consider how you achieve them and where they rank on your importance scale.

Are they more important than your health, relationships, service to others, and growth? Don't get me wrong; having goals and a vision is excellent, I have mine. I'm just asking you a few questions to determine whether you think you might benefit from some awareness.

Truth Takes Work

Living your truth rarely "just happens" magically. You must do the work. How? Yes, great question. First, you must locate a list of human values. I recommend looking at the work of Brené Brown, who has done wonderful work and research around values. You can find out more and do the work here at the website in the footnote.[2]

The exercise I lead participants through in my workshops focuses on engaging with your values through what I call the 3 Rs:

- Recognize

- Review

- Reflect

Start by creating a table (on paper or on your computer) that is four columns wide labeled as shown in the graphic, then complete using the instructions below.

MY VALUES (Live Your Truth)	SELF-RATING (1 LO to 10 HI)	WHAT GETS IN THE WAY?	I WILL … (ACTIONS)

Recognize

I advise you to develop a list of values, making sure all of them truly resonate with you. You may have 8, 14, or 23. There is no "right" number. The number is the number. Once you have these, I like to list them in the left-hand column of your 4-column table.

---

2 https://brenebrown.com/resources/living-into-our-values/

Review

This step is essential to ensure you are living your values. To do that, you must review them consistently. I recommend once a week. Set a recurring meeting on your calendar. (Friday mornings work for me.) In the second column from the left, assign a 1-10 rating to each of the values: 1 is low meaning you're not doing a good job of living that value; 10 is perfection. I never have a 10, as I believe I can always live more strongly and courageously into my values. (You outstanding accountants can use decimal places if needed.)

The third column is titled *What gets in the way?* This is where you do the work to identify challenges and blocks . . . and a lot of excuses for why a rating of one of your values is lower than you'd like it to be.

The fourth column is the most important, resulting from completing the first three. It is titled "I will . . . (Actions)." This is where you identify specific actions you can take in the next week(s) to bring you back into balance with your values and allow you to live your truth more authentically.

At the top of the next page is an example of how I reviewed myself on a few of my values.

Reflect

This final stage of the 3Rs is the time you spend thinking about where you are and where you're headed. This is the time to reflect and focus on the bigger picture and do it with a peaceful perspective. Be grateful for the areas of your life where you are living your

MY VALUES (Live Your Truth)	SELF-RATING (1 LO to 10 HI)	WHAT GETS IN THE WAY?	I WILL ... (ACTIONS)
Faith	8	• Time • Excuses • Lack of focus • Mindset	• Meditate more • Develop faith talk • "Give" • Daily mass 2x week • Study more • Keynote
Family & Friends Commitment • Husband • Father • Son • Brother • Friend • Human	7	• Lack of focus / plan • Delay having tough conversations • Fear • "Busy"	• 1 on 1 time with kids • Visits with Trish • Call / text 4 people weekly • Focus on the good in people • Appreciate Lisa • Mom/dad weekly visit
Health	8	• Time • Lack of intention • Diet—lack of focus	• Mix routine & exercises • Envision diet—food/ alcohol • **Run 3x week—sunrise** • Meditate
Growth / Optimism	7	• The past • Comparing to others • Negative people • $$$ • Crappy self-talk • Mindset	• Journal & Meditate • Read 2 books/month • Watch / listen / learn • Schedule solo retreat

values. Be gentle with yourself—or pissed off, whichever emotion gets the job done—about the areas where you need to focus and do the work to enhance the level of living your truth. You'll be glad you did.

Balance is not a value: *If I had a dollar every time someone said to me, "I need more balance," I'd have a lot of dollars. Balance is often listed as a value, and I disagree. Balance, this sought-after nirvana, is your state of existence, your engagement with the world when your value ratings are where you desire them to be. I believe balance is the result of doing the above exercise over and over again . . . always* *focused and working on getting your value ratings to where you want them to be . . . then, voilá . . . you experience more balance in your life. All by simply living your truth.*

Am I Living My Truth?

When you live your truth and continuously pursue your authentic self:

- You do what brings you joy

- You're not swayed, influenced, or angered by the opinions of others

- You do not need validation from others . . . your validation is internal

- You don't take things personally

- You accept others living their truths

- You are "more than" your job or position or title

- You experience "balance" as you define it

- You move toward the end of your life without regret . . . you live with grace

Living your truth is an essential ingredient of **arrfYl**. Perhaps this quote from the Stoic philosopher Epictetus captures what I'm working to explain...

"You can always win if you only enter competitions where winning is up to you."

When you get clear on your values and your thoughts and actions are consistent with them . . . when you live YOUR truth . . . you win.

Live your truth.

#3

LOVE YOUR PEOPLE FIERCELY ... and LET THEM LOVE YOU

"Love is the condition in which the happiness of another person is essential to your own."

— Robert Heinlein

Love Your People Fiercely ... and Let Them Love You!

Read the quote on the previous page again. Do you agree? I sure do. I came across this quote randomly and knew it might fit somewhere in this book, and I believe it's here . . . where you have the choice to take your people and relationships for granted . . . or to love your people fiercely.

When you live with **arrfYl**, you know your relationships are ultimately your trustworthy source of fulfillment and resilience. There are other things like money, houses, and cars and . . . well, you know what I mean. Ultimately, though, it's all about your relationships. You read in Chapter 1 how your relationship with Spirit is the strength of your foundation. Add to this your relationships with family and friends, and your foundation for living with **arrfYl** and being fully alive will grow stronger.

How are you doing with loving your people . . . fiercely? Fiercely is a great word, isn't it? Fiercely means *with a heartfelt and powerful intensity.* Perhaps ask yourself this question more consistently: *Do I love my people fiercely?* The actions we take because of the questions we ask ourselves—and answer—are fertile ground for growth and fulfillment.

Fierce Love in the Blue Zone

If you're unfamiliar with "blue zones," I recommend spending time on the bluezones.com website. Blue zones is a concept developed in 2004 by Dan Buettner, a National Geographic Explorer, after he had visited Okinawa, Japan, to investigate longevity and then explored other regions with high longevity and life satisfaction. He and his research found five areas around the globe where people seemed to live longer and with a better quality of life than the general population.

One key aspect of blue zones is the relationship between the people. Here's a quote from the blue zones website:

> *In Okinawa, Japan, a blue zones area where people live longer, healthier lives, they create small groups called "moais." A moai is a circle of friends who support and encourage each other through life.*

A moai (pronounced mo-eye) is a lifelong circle of friends where people provide varying forms of support for social, financial, health, or spiritual interests. Moai means "meeting for a common purpose" in Japanese. This common purpose is synonymous with what I believe you're here to create, experience for yourself, and support and appreciate others to do the same...fulfillment and resilience.

I got to experience the principle of moai in action on a recent family trip to Italy. My wife, Lisa, and I had decided to go away with our children to celebrate turning 60, our 30th wedding anniversary, and our youngest, Lizzy, graduating college. We spent a few days in Dublin, Ireland, then went to Italy for almost two weeks. We stayed together in rented homes, and my favorite was a top-floor, two-story apartment with a massive outdoor tiled patio overlooking Marina Grande in Sorrento. (Google Marina Grande Sorrento to see this special place.)

The building was perched atop a cliff over the marina, and you could access it either by road or by foot via an ancient Grecian pathway winding down a natural wall of rock. It was simply amazing.

Our hosts were two Italian sisters, Filomena, and Angela. They were married to men who'd been best friends since childhood, Franco and Luigi.

As you might imagine, these women are excellent cooks. You could hire them to come to the apartment and cook dinner and have it served it on the sizeable tile-floored balcony overlooking the marina and facing west to watch the soul-stirring scene of the sun dropping into the Tyrrhenian Sea.

We unanimously agreed we needed to do this and enjoyed an incredibly fresh and delicious meal of eggplant, fish, pasta, salad, prosciutto, cheeses, and dessert. To top it off, Franco arrived at dessert time with homemade limoncello. We all toasted one another, and Franco talked with me in broken English about growing up in Sorrento, being friends with Luigi, marrying Filomena, and Luigi marrying Angela. It was good that he knew English as my Italian was limited. At one point, he pointed to some small wooden tables sitting beside the ancient stone wall leading to the clear waters below. I knew those tables since I had used one the day before while enjoying a cold beer. He talked about how each night he, Luigi, and a few other friends gathered around the tables to spend time together and enjoy some wine, some limoncello… and most importantly…each other. They recount their days, share joys, sadness, achievements, and setbacks, and make fun of one another lovingly and playfully.

Franco paused, looked down to the marina, then back to me with misty eyes, and said in broken English, "It is good for us. Friendship, it is…" he squinted, searching his English vocabulary for the word, "it is *positivo*."

Yes, positivo indeed! I'm unsure if Franco ever read The Top 5 Regrets of the Dying, although I am sure he'll not regret this one…I wish I had stayed in touch with my friends.

We hugged, and I agreed with him. Loving your people fiercely is indeed positivo. It should be a primary focus when you get your ass out of bed each day. Pay attention to your moai and love your people fiercely…Franco sure does.

Letting Your Moai In

Being part of a moai is a two-way street. You must be present in the lives of the people you love, *and* you must let your moai love and support you.

I learned the vital importance of reciprocity only long after my electrocution accident. At that time, I did *not* let my moai, my people, in. I did not allow them to support me; I did not let them love me fiercely. I had my mom, dad, one sister, six brothers (yes, a sort of Catholic version of Snow White), my three best friends, and my then-girlfriend, Lisa, all passionately committed to loving and supporting me. So why, then, did I shut them out and refuse the healing energy they offered? Because in my muddled mindset, full of pain and blame, despair and shitty self-esteem, I believed they did not know what I was going through.

And I was right, they didn't. How could they? They never had electricity travel through their body and blow holes in their feet, socks, and boots in its need to exit their body. They never stared into the blank eyes of a friend and performed CPR, and all you wanted was for him to f**king breathe again.

Here's the thing, though: I was not right; I was very wrong in my assessment of them. When your moai wants to love and support you, it's best to enter the world of your vulnerability and let them. Don't let your vulnerability and opportunity for solid connection lie dormant beneath your wounded emotional surface. Healing will not take place. You'll stay stuck. Instead, take a breath, trust, and open up. When you're struggling, do not be so concerned with what your Moai says; be thankful they showed up for you and said something. This is their way of loving you fiercely. Make sense?

Historically, the moai tradition in Japan was treated formally, with children paired up in groups of five and expected to make a lifelong commitment to each other. In today's mobile society, that kind of constancy of contact is rare, but I love the general idea of defining and appreciating the people who make up your closest and strongest support network. So stop reading right now and think about or make a list of your moai. Who are the people who love you fiercely and whom you love fiercely? They want the best for you always. And vice versa. They'll challenge you and call b.s. on you when needed. And you'll do the same for them.

Now raise your hand if you need to spend more time with them and love them more . . . fiercely. Excellent, well done. You can put your hand down now. Stop reading again and text, call, or send a selfie video to let them know how much they mean in your life and how much you *appreciate* them.

Appreciation as an Expression of Love

Dr. William James is often referred to as the founder of American psychology. He taught his first experimental psychology course at Harvard in the 1875–1876 academic year and spoke one of my favorite quotes:

> *"The deepest principle in human nature is the craving to be appreciated."*

I think Dan Buettner uncovered proof of the truth of Dr. James' statement when he learned about the moai.

John Mackey, the founder and former CEO of Whole Foods Market, believes love and appreciation are at the core of building an organization's culture. The company implemented the practice of ending every meeting with an appreciation. He said people must be connected to a purpose *and* know they are loved and appreciated. He wrote a great book titled *Conscious Leadership* and believed "LOVE is the best leadership strategy."

"LOVE is the best leadership strategy."

Being from Philadelphia and a sports fan (and please, no Dallas Cowboys comments), I saw the power of this appreciation principle played out with Trea Turner, the shortstop for the Philadelphia Phillies. Going into August of 2023, Turner was struggling at the plate with his hitting, with a dismal average of just .235.

Up until that point, the fans had regularly booed Turner. But that all changed at his first at-bat on August 4th, when the crowd instead gave him a standing ovation (you can watch it at the link in the footnote[3]). In the week after the ovation, Turner's batting average was .370, with two home runs, four doubles, and eight RBIs. The Phillies finished the season strong, though ultimately lost to the Arizona Diamondbacks in game 7 of the National League Championship Season. Turner went to the All-Star Game in 2024; at that time, his batting average was .349.

Loving Others Helps You

Desiree Linden won the 2018 Boston Marathon in some of the worst weather in race history. She was the first American woman to win the race in over 30 years. What I found interesting in an article about Linden's stunning victory is how it connected to loving your people fiercely.[4]

---

3 https://x.com/NBCSPhilly/status/1687609727545425923?ref_src=
twsrc%5Etfw%7Ctwcamp%5Etweetembed%7Ctwterm%5E168760
9727545425923%7Ctwgr%5E592005c6dcc0e08fe9cb21b36406ba7
de1a42e45%7Ctwcon%5Es1_c10&ref_url=https%3A%2F%2Fwww.
washingtonpost.com%2Fsports%2F2023%2F10%2F04%2Ft
rea-turner-ovation-phillies%2F

4 https://www.runnersworld.com/training/a19862759/
sportsmanship-desiree-linden-boston-marathon/

One of the favorites to win the race was fellow American Shalane Flanagan. Linden was not feeling well early in the race. "Early on, I was feeling horrible," Linden said. "I gave Shalane a tap and said, 'There's a really good chance I'm going to drop out today. If you need anything—block the wind, adjust the pace maybe—let me know.'"

Around the halfway point of the race, Flanagan took a bathroom break, and Linden slowed down so she could pace Flanagan to get back to the front-pack of elite runners. What happened next is interesting.

"When you work together, you never know what's gonna happen," Linden said. "Helping her helped me, and I kind of got my legs back from there." She won the Boston Marathon.

Nicole Detling, Ph.D., sports psychologist, explains what happened and perhaps why Linden won. "Your brain releases endorphins, dopamine, and serotonin when you help someone." These neurotransmitters are valuable in a race and everyday life. According to the Hawaii Medical Journal, endorphins have a way of reducing pain, dopamine increases motivation and focus, and serotonin boosts your mood. Detling summed it up, "I have no doubt that this surge of hormones helped Linden turn the race around."

What I found powerful in the quote above is where Detling mentions the power of these neurotransmitters *in everyday life.*

See the footnote for a link to a summary of Linden's magical race.[5]

---

5 https://www.youtube.com/watch?v=BfmI6gIk2IY

Living With Fierce Love

I met a young man years ago whose story will stay with me forever. He was battling cancer . . . and he was amazing.

I met him when I volunteered for a wish-granting organization where my partner and I would visit a sick child and his/her family and gather information about them and a wish they'd like to receive.

We learned he was a 12-year-old with a twin brother and a younger sister. His parents were getting divorced, and he and his siblings were living with their mother at a relative's crowded home. Upon meeting him, I was moved by his energy and optimistic nature. He was a quiet young man who loved basketball, and he and I spent time together in the driveway shooting hoops.

His cancer was in his lower leg, so a wish involving significant travel was not possible for him and his family. He would eventually have his leg amputated below the knee. His wish was to go on a shopping spree. He and his family would be picked up in a limousine, I'd follow in my pick-up truck with room for all the purchases, and we'd end the day with a great dinner.

He received $150 x his age, so that was $1,800. My wonderful wish-granting partner and I got another $400 in gift cards from generous retailers . . . so this young man had $2,200 to spend. Our first stop was Dick's Sporting Goods. He was more reserved than usual and was not spending any money. Wait, correction: he spent some money as soon as we arrived. He told his brother and sister to each pick out a pair of sneakers . . . and he would buy them—part one of the lesson this wise young man was offering me.

I talked with him and told him we needed to spend some money because we "didn't have all day." It was not the best communication for me, talking to a kid with cancer about time. I'd reword that if I had another chance. We looked at new basketball hoops because the one he had at his relatives' house was old and rickety and would often blow over with a strong wind. I told him he had plenty of money to get this, we could load it into my truck, and I'd come to the house with my tools to mount it to the driveway so it would be solid. He smiled and said, "Yeah, maybe."

At this point, I playfully hugged and shook him gently, saying, "Dude, you gotta spend some money." He said he'd find his sister and brother and tell them about the basketball hoop.

I went to find his mother, a young woman immersed in her strenuous struggle of a nasty divorce and her quest to heal her sick child. I found her mindlessly looking through a clothes rack. Our conversation went like this:

Me: Hi

Her: Hi.

Me: How are you doing?

Her: OK, I guess.

Me: You know he's not spending money. Is he OK?

She was quiet and looked down to the floor.

Me: What is it? Please talk to me.

Her: Well, it's just that I asked him this morning if he was excited, and he . . . he . . .

Me: He what?

Her: He said, I am Mom, but this is a lot of money, and I want to make sure you are alright.

I took a deep breath as the silence settled, and I processed part two of the lesson my young friend was teaching me. Remember the quote from the beginning of this chapter: *Love is the condition in which the happiness of another person is essential to your own.* I hugged her, told her I understood, and thanked her for telling me. I then went and found him and explained that he didn't have to spend all the money, just what he felt comfortable with. He smiled, and I could see a weight lifted for him. He bought himself some sneakers, athletic clothing, and sports jerseys and got something for his mom. When he asked if I wanted anything, I smiled and said, "No, thanks, I'm good." Little did he know the great gift he had already given me.

We left and went to a few other stores where he got some things. We finished the day with a beautiful meal, and he went home with money still in his pocket. It was a day I cherish. My young friend lived with **arrfYl**; he did not let his illness and cancer shatter his Soul.

My young friend lived with arrfYl; he did not let his illness and cancer shatter his Soul.

My young friend knew one of his values was to love his people fiercely . . . and he did. I was told a few years later he had lost his battle with cancer. I think of him often.

Leave the Sandbags Behind

One last thought in this chapter: We should all learn to love ourselves just as fiercely as we love others! That means letting go of your regrets and negative experiences so you can live and love fully in the moment.

Years ago, I sat on the beach in Cape May, NJ, and watched a mother with two young girls arrive and set up their beach camp. It was cute to see the girls helping their mom fill the not-so-small sandbags and then clip one to each of the four strings on each corner of the canopy to anchor it against the wind. I guess each sandbag weighed about ten pounds.

A few hours later, the husband/father arrived and played with the girls for hours—a good man indeed. He dug holes, let them bury him, rode waves with them, and shared a few snacks.

The girls got restless, and the mom took them off the beach as I watched the dad break down the camp. I chuckled when he loaded the four sandbags into his beach cart along with chairs, boogie boards, blankets, and buckets and struggled to drag the cart across the hot, soft sand.

I wanted to run to the guy, hug him, and say, "Hey, brother, how about you and I empty out the sandbags . . . because I'm pretty sure there will be more sand here tomorrow."

This story works as a metaphor for so many people I've met in my life, including myself at times Each day, we fill our bags with guilt, blame, regret, despair, and other negative energies, and we pack it up and carry it around for months, years, some for their entire life. Look, you and me, we all make mistakes. At the end of your day, empty your "sand bags." Hit your knees, say a prayer, smile, give yourself a hug, and get back after life tomorrow. It is powerful to love your people fiercely, and don't stop there . . . *also, love yourself fiercely!*

Lead With Love

While the majority—maybe all— of you have not stood in a Major League batting box or won the Boston Marathon, nor, I hope, have faced a terminal cancer diagnosis, you all have the opportunity each day to do what I call "LWL" . . . lead with love. The people in your life need you, and you need them. Think about how you support them. Think about how you stay by their side when they need to "get back in the race" or "hit a homer." The strangers you encounter daily are also strong candidates for your love, care, and compassion. Be on the lookout for them; you have no idea the brutal race they may be running in their life and how your love and kindness may be just what they need. When you love your people fiercely, you:

- Know your happiness depends on theirs

- Are intentional about your focus on your relationships

- Let them love you back

- Know the "positivo" available through healthy relationships

- Empty your own sandbags.

Love your people . . . fiercely . . . and let them love you the same way. Deal?

#4

TRUST YOU ARE A RESILIENT HUMAN BEING

"For scientific discovery, give me Scott;
for speed and efficiency of travel, give me Amundsen.
But when disaster strikes and all hope is gone,
get down on your knees and pray for Shackleton."

—Sir Raymond Priestly, Antarctic Explorer

Trust You Are a Resilient Human Being

Irishman Sir Earnest Shackleton was an Antarctic explorer in the early 1900s and an often studied and quoted figure on leadership. When I first read of his ill-fated expedition on the wooden ship in 1914, I was struck by his innate sense of resilience, his deep knowing that if one just keeps going, they will endure. He is also known for his ability to influence others to believe in their resilience—their ability to endure difficulties in life. I guess this is called leadership, right?

Shackleton departed on December 5, 1914. His goal on this expedition was to sail with his 27-man crew to the Weddell Sea and then be the first to cross the Antarctic continent via the pole. He had failed to reach the pole on a previous expedition in 1909, coming up just 97 miles short.

He and his men were focused on going to the bottom of the Earth, the least-known part of the world where temperatures plummeted to -70 degrees and the wind howled at 100 miles per hour. I guess we can deduce that Shackleton's dharma—his truth, his reality—was to lead men to explore the unknown, and his passion for this was intense.

The ship encountered packs of ice in the sea, slowing its progress until, on January 19, 1915, it became trapped in the ice like a leaf on a frozen pond. Shackleton ordered the abandonment of the ship on February 24th after realizing it would be trapped in the ice until Spring. The men set up camp on the ice and waited. When Spring came, the ship floated with the ice over the summer until it was crushed, taking in water in October and ultimately sinking to the bottom of the sea on November 21, 1915.

This, for me, is when the test of survival—and the vital need for resilience and a positive mindset—*really* began for Shackleton. I mean, I can imagine him and his men were concerned before this, but now? Now, your ship was at the bottom of the ocean.

Shackleton and his men set up camp and drifted on ice flows, with Shackleton "trusting" they'd float to Paulet Island, 250 miles away, where it was known that supplies were stored. This did not happen. On April 9th, their ice flow broke, and Shackleton ordered his men into the three lifeboats they'd rescued from the ship and head to the nearest land. After five brutal days, with the men tired, freezing, and wet . . . they landed on Elephant Island. *It was the first time they stood on land in 497 days!* Can you imagine not being on solid land for over a year and four months? Elephant Island was far from shipping routes, and Shackleton knew rescue was unlikely.

Shackleton was a man who knew he was a resilient human being. He knew he must take a few men and set out to South Georgia Island, a 720-nautical-mile open sea voyage . . . in a 20-foot lifeboat. When you trust you're a resilient human being, you know the power of taking action. There is no resilience where there is no action. He chose five men to accompany him on this journey and packed supplies for only four weeks, knowing they would perish if they did not reach their destination in that time frame.

They launched on April 24, 1916, and for the next 15 days, were at the mercy of the mighty ocean and in constant danger of capsizing. The good news is that on May 8th, they landed on one side of South Georgia island

The bad news was that they landed on the wrong side —the inhabited Norwegian whaling station was located on the other side. After a few days of rest and knowing the lifeboat was not fit for another sea journey, Shackleton took two of the men and set off on a land crossing to the whaling station. Again, notice the action. The trek would be thirty-two miles over ice—and snow-covered mountains known as the Southern Alps. The men had pushed screws through their boots to act as climbing boots and had a 50-foot rope and a carpenter's adze, a tool for scraping and smoothing wood. Thirty-six hours later, they arrived at the whaling station on May 20th, 1916. Shackleton returned to rescue all his men.

The next successful crossing of South Georgia Island was in 1955 by British explorer Duncan Carse, who traveled much the same route as Shackleton. When asked about Shackleton's crossing, he says, "I do not know how they did it, except that they had to."

**"I do not know how they did it,
except that they had to."**

Many consider Shackleton's story one of the greatest survival stories in history, which I could have used in the first chapter. Remember the title: Be More Spirit.

Sir Earnest Shackleton trusted in his Spirit and the Spirit of his men. He worked to influence his men to connect with the energy of their own Spirit . . . and *trust they were resilient human beings!* The definition of resilient is *able to withstand or recover quickly from difficult conditions.* I'd likely challenge the use of the word quickly in this definition as I've experienced and seen others "stay in the struggle" with courage and finally come out on the other side. Some of life's shitshows can last awhile. The residue from my accident hung around for 20+ years, continuing to show up as my "demons" and working to beat me down.

The name of Shackleton's ship? Would you believe it was named *Endurance*? I don't think that name is a coincidence. Resilience and endurance are closely related mindsets . . . it is all about the internal voice that says, "keep going." In fact, I don't believe in coincidences. I agree with Albert Einstein when he offered this insight: "Coincidences are God's way of remaining anonymous." Yes, right on Albert.

As I've come to understand it, resilience should also include "connect with your Spirit" in its definition. So, how's this for a definition of resilience: *the ability to connect with your Spirit to withstand and recover from one of life's inevitable struggles or shitshows.* Use it if you'd like.

Change Yourself When You Can't Change the Situation

The key to having a resilient mindset is not to discount the brutal facts of a bad situation you find yourself in. Instead, acknowledge them and deal with them. Monitor your thoughts, always catch the negative ones, and have a strategy to convert them to positive, optimistic ones. Shackleton knew one of life's basic principles: *the best way to change a situation is to change yourself in it.* Let me offer it again: **the best way to change a situation is to change yourself in it.**

You must surrender to the circumstances as they *are.* But you do not have to surrender to them *staying that way.* Surrendering to your circumstances can build momentum to move you forward.

You may be asking yourself now, "Danny, how can surrendering build momentum?" and I understand. When you surrender, and accept the reality of your situation then you can shift your focus from where you are . . . to the vision of where you are headed. Then figure out the next action to take to move forward. I've seen too many people stuck, without momentum, because their focus is on where they are. This surrender is definitely not from your place of weakness . . . rather, it is from your place of strength, wisdom and commitment to move forward.

Your change and growth are rooted in changing your perspective, judgment, and how you think about your situation. Too many people continue to focus on and invest energy in the facts they have no control over.

Shackleton and his men dealt with the brutal facts of the rough ocean, beat-up boats, challenging climate, and the lack of food, clothing, and shelter. He did not lack a strong and trusting connection with his Spirit. **This trust in his Spiritual nature triumphed over the forces of Mother Nature.**

Positive thinking plays a crucial role in building resilience by shaping how we perceive and respond to challenges. Being positive makes you more resilient in the following ways:

- **Setbacks are seen as temporary**: Positive thinking encourages an outlook of trust, which helps with the belief that setbacks can be overcome. This optimism makes setbacks seem more like temporary obstacles rather than permanent failures.

- **Reducing stress**: Focusing on the positive aspects of a situation makes it easier to stay calm and think clearly, which are essential for making decisions in tough situations. That's not to say you won't experience any stress, but with a positive attitude the stress can be less intense or shorter-lived than you might otherwise experience.

- **Improving creativity**: Positive thinking enhances creative thinking and problem-solving abilities. When people believe in the possibility of positive outcomes, they are more likely to seek solutions rather than dwell on problems.

- **Increasing confidence in your ability**: Positive thinking fosters confidence in one's abilities, helping people feel empowered to tackle challenges head-on. This belief in oneself is a core component of resilience.

- **Improving your relationships**: Positive thinking often leads to better interpersonal relationships, providing a supportive social network, which is a key factor in resilience. Surrounding yourself with positivity helps buffer the impact of hardships.

Together, these factors create a feedback loop where positive thinking strengthens resilience, and resilience, in turn, reinforces the ability to maintain positivity in the face of adversity.

Discovering Resilience

On January 1, 2023, Jeremy Renner, the actor famous for his role as an Avenger, was crushed by a snow plow, leaving him with 38 broken bones, his eyeball out of his head, and mangled legs. His story and recovery is impressive, and I gained value and validation when I heard his insight on the Late Night Show with Jimmy Fallon when he said,

> *"I won't have a bad day for the rest of my life. It's impossible. Right? There's that gift."*

He was also a guest on the Smartless podcast, and the following is from the transcript.

> *"The exhilarating peace that happens, you know in you know leaving this body . . . and it's f**king exhilarating as it is peaceful there's nothing to freaking worry about at the end of the day um you know and I can confirm that we all have something to look forward to um whether we use God to get there right or whatever it is but it's something to look forward to and it's Blissful it's beautiful and um there's accountability and responsibility that comes along with it . . .*
> *"*

Jeremy Renner lives with **arrfY1** and certainly is a living testament to this chapter's title: *Trust You are a Resilient Human Being*. He just committed to "keep going."

Where in your past have you been resilient? Did you trust you were a resilient person? Did you believe you had "no choice in the matter" and stayed in the struggle until it was over? If you haven't, this is okay. Many of us—me for sure—have said, "I don't know how I'm going to get through this" or some similar statement. What's important is that the residue of the times you have not been resilient does not influence and impact your future. You must get good at learning from the past and not allowing the residue to exist. Take a breath, learn and move on.

The foundation for your resilience and trust in your ability to get through "anything" is often laid during your struggles in life. They may come early in life; they may not come until later. My life was void of any significant struggle until my accident at 28 years old. It laid a massively strong foundation for my resilience, although I did not realize it for many years. Subsequent struggles I've endured of job loss, relationship issues, loss of loved ones, and others have continued to strengthen this foundation. And, of course, my moai (remember that) is a significant part of my resilience foundation.

Trust you are a resilient human being . . . because you are . . . it's your birthright.

#5

EMBRACE THE STRUGGLE

Although the world is full of suffering,
it is also full of overcoming it.

—Helen Keller

Embrace the Struggle

When I was in grade school, I learned about Helen Keller and her amazing life after losing her eyesight and hearing at 19 months old. Keller became a world-famous speaker and author, traveling to twenty-five countries to deliver motivational speeches, and she published 12 books. I recall the impact on me and my classmates when our teacher experimented with us. She made us close our eyes and put cotton in our ears for a few minutes. I was probably only 11 years old or so. She made us all aware of the gift of our sight and hearing, and I'm sure that long ago contributed to the foundation of what has become my life philosophy of living with **arrfYl**, thanks to a curious teacher and the inspiring Helen Keller, who ultimately embraced her struggle and lived with **arrfYl**.

Perhaps that's also why I take inspiration from Keller's quote at the opening of this chapter. I witness people daily who prove it. Let me explain how I use the word embrace for this principle. The definition is *to accept or support (a belief, theory, or change) willingly and enthusiastically.* I pull out of this definition these two words: *accept* and *willingly.* You'll recall *radical* means very different from the usual and traditional, and "embracing the struggle" connects with that idea.

For most people faced with a tragedy, struggle, or setback, their first thought is not radical. It's not this, "OK, great. I am going to EMBRACE this." Instead, the first responses are ones

I have experienced many times, and I'm sure you have also. They are usual and traditional:

I can't believe this.

How will I ever get through this?

This sucks.

This is not fair.

What did I do to deserve this?

Right? I know these statements are true because after my life-changing accident, I did not *embrace the struggle.* Quite the opposite. I blamed myself for not paying enough attention to the electric line strung innocently between two wooden poles, and I blamed God for letting this happen and for losing Bruce that day. I began to understand the need to embrace the struggle and acknowledge the brutal facts just a bit when I walked out of the phone booth in the Outer Banks after a brief call with my mom when I was drunk.

For the first time since the accident, I embraced the shitty facts of life I was challenged to overcome. I was not thrilled, excited, or delighted with them; I just embraced them . . . I accepted them willingly. Then, I began to get just the smallest amount of traction to move forward to get better and heal. It did not happen overnight, and accepting the facts and surrendering to their reality was the shift that began moving me forward.

The Latin phrase, *amor fati,* translates to "surrender to fate." This is the foundation for embracing the struggle; it is a vital part of living with **arrfY1** and is often overlooked by many in the shitshows and struggles of their life. People usually think they are—or should be—insulated from suffering and struggle when it is really a fertile space for growth and filling your reservoir of resilience. God, or the Universe or whatever name you may give our human Higher Power, is not up there behind the curtain like the Wizard of Oz, pulling the strings and cranking levers to make bad things happen to us.

Events are neutral; it's your perspective that gives them meaning. This can be tough to grasp. No one wants "bad" things to happen, although the Stoic philosopher Seneca thought differently. He believed misfortune was inevitable in life and a good thing, as moving through it makes you stronger and more of who you were born to be.

"I judge you unfortunate because you have never lived through misfortune. You have passed through life without an opponent—no one can ever know what you are capable of, not even you."

Events are neutral; it's your perspective that gives them meaning.

Getting to the mindset of embracing your struggle will likely take time. How long? Up to you. I hope you'll find inspiration in this chapter to help.

Obstacles and Opportunities

Ryan Holiday, whom I mentioned before, wrote a book I've recommended to you. It's titled *The Obstacle Is the Way*. The book is about how Stoic philosophers in ancient Greece saw their obstacles as opportunities for growth and resilience and how we should ultimately focus on controlling what we can control. You cannot control tragedy and struggle; you can only control how you respond with your thoughts and actions.

The book has been published in 40 languages and has sold over 2 million copies in English. NBA, NFL, and PGA champions have heralded it as supporting them in reframing their challenges in sports . . .and life.

Ryan Shazier is a former linebacker for the Pittsburgh Steelers who sustained an on-field spinal injury that left him unable to walk. He talked about how *The Obstacle Is the Way* helped him strengthen his mindset and the positive focus it created for his recovery. The book is a powerful source of support when facing a struggle, and life may seem to be "winning."

I believe one of the most brutal struggles to face, embrace, and ultimately move through is the loss of a child. I've witnessed it several times with friends, and it rips my heart apart. I cannot imagine what it does to theirs. I've seen the suffering and sadness that is their constant companion, and then I've seen them slowly move to a state of healing. Oh, they never forget, and the pain lingers . . . it's just they heal and continue in life, and they inspire me.

Again, I don't know if the strong people I know ever used the word *embrace* as they dealt with their loss. They did come to operate from a mindset with a synonymous description of the embrace concept. They said things like . . .

"We're fighting the fight."

"We will not give up."

"We must press on."

"We're just focused on one day at a time."

These people will never forget their child, and the pain lingers always, a dull ache sometimes, a violent intruder of pain at other times. Yet they persist. They work themselves back to the life where joy and laughter and the simple appreciation of this gift called life reside. I prayed with them and for them and talked with them for hours.

When any great tragedy comes, most of us believe the world's greatest lie: fate has taken over, and we are powerless. We must realize this frame of mind, this defeated attitude . . .is the *world's greatest lie,* as described in the beautiful book *The Alchemist* by Paulo Coelho. It's another one of my favorite books, offering the reader much introspection about their life and continued growth. When the main character, a young shepherd named Santiago, asks a mysterious old man, "What's the world's greatest lie?" the old man replies:

"It's this: that at a certain point in our lives, we lose control of what's happening to us, and our lives become controlled by fate. That's the world's greatest lie."

My friends inspire me. The pain hangs around, yet these people—and you as well—grow to embrace life after the loss, and the fact you can move on . . . and honor them by living with **arrfYl**.

Embrace the Suck

I met Darleen Santore, known as "Coach Dar," when I asked her to be a guest on my Back to Life podcast. She's a fantastic woman with a powerful story of resilience. She went in one day for a routine chiropractic adjustment, and a blood vessel in her brain ruptured. This led to three life-threatening strokes, the last one leaving her unable to speak, and the doctors said she may die at any time.

Coach Dar speaks about the need to "embrace the suck" when . . . when . . . well . . . when life sucks. You should google her, listen to some of her insight on resilience, and get her book if you're a reader. It's titled, *The Art of Bouncing Back: Find Your Flow to Thrive at Work and in Life—Any Time You're Off Your Game.*

I researched this phrase, *embrace the suck*, and it seems it is a military phrase that became popular during the Iraq War in 2003. I've seen it attributed to both the Navy SEALs and the Marines. The source is less important than the powerful mental energy this phrase creates when internalized. It means *accepting the uncomfortable things and situations in life and confronting them to take action to make them better.*

Over the years, with our three kids, I've often been confronted with the phrase, "Dad, you don't understand; this sucks."

I usually pause, then agree with them, as the facts are what they are, and it does suck.

I then offer my kid a simple question consistent with the mindset of embracing the suck. I offer them this: "What's it going to be like when it doesn't suck?" I encourage you to stay aware of the power of this question and ask it of yourself when needed. I've seen it create an instant shift for many people. For the parents who lose a child, it may never not suck, as the loss is the most vicious void created in one's life . . . and I do believe and have seen many who surrender and embrace their life without their child . . . and they press on.

Shaping the Voices in Your Head

I've come to understand this: *your life is lived between your ears!*

Young monk. Used with permission.

A voice in your head (sometimes a few!) results from interpreting all the inputs you experience. This voice(s) forms your mindset and attitude in life. It puts words and language into our interpretations and becomes our thoughts and story. It is this voice that either tells you to embrace the suck and move through it, or to bitch and slide into the valley of the victim, a place of increased pain, no movement forward, despair, and lack of Faith.

After my accident, I took up "residence" in the *valley of the victim*. The valley of the victim is the mental state of mind when you are not moving forward. You believe life is not fair, "this" should not have happened, and you just cannot seem to understand that life unfolds and struggles arrive. When you do get to understand that life unfolds and struggles arise and no one is exempt of them, and shit just happens . . . well, then you begin to shift your mindset and there is a mental momentum created, which leads to action and movement forward.

To avoid or escape the valley of the victim, we can turn to that trait of resilience, which I discussed earlier. Here's another example of resilience: A treasure hunter named Mel Fisher and his team found one of the greatest treasures from the sea. He searched for the treasure of the 1622 wreck of the Nuestra Señora de Atocha in Florida waters for 16 years, from 1969 until 1985. Then the voice of Mel's son, Kane, came over the radio and said, "Put away the charts. We've found the main pile."

Mel and his crew recovered over $450 million of gold, silver, and emeralds. I found two things interesting about Mel and his long journey to find the treasure. The first is the struggle and setbacks he endured with the weather, lawsuits, financial struggle, and the tragic loss of his son, his daughter-in-law, and another diver when a boat capsized. He had dozens of reasons to give up. But he didn't.

The second is what he said to himself each morning, what the voice in his head said. It said this:

"Today's the day."

Having never talked to Mel Fisher, I can't say for sure that he ever "embraced the suck," but he sure didn't let it stop him. I have to believe that what kept him going was that he trusted he was a resilient human being quite capable of handling the setbacks and struggles he encountered. You can do the same.

I like using acronyms in my writing and speaking. For me, and maybe you, they are remembered easier, and often, just saying or recalling the acronym can quickly communicate the entire concept. It can provide a quick and powerful shift in your attitude and energy. One of my favorites is H.U.T. It stands for "hold useful thoughts."

You see, your thoughts create the emotions you feel, which drive your actions. You rarely act from logic. Have you ever done something you later deemed not a good choice, only to ask yourself in reflection, "What was I thinking?" The fact is you weren't. At least not thinking logically. Your thoughts created an emotional state from which you acted and produced the outcome.

What you say to yourself must elicit a strong emotion of focus, resilience, joy, or the like so you take an action likely to produce your desired outcome. It is a simple concept, it just takes a solid awareness to think this way. You must become very good at self-coaching and monitoring what's being said in your head. You must build strong mental habits like the Stoics and others I've mentioned. After my accident things changed when I no longer blamed my self, or told myself I did not deserve to be happy.

When Mel said, "Today's the day," every day for 16 years, I am confident it put him and his team into a positive emotional state of resilience, commitment, and respect for each other. They went out to the waters to continue their search. It's the same for you. What are you searching for? What do you want to create? What new things do you need to say to yourself to get to the emotion needed to take action?

Be Lost . . . Just Don't Stay There

The idea that we "get up on the wrong side of the bed" is a convenient way to blame external factors for our mood, but the truth runs deeper. We don't wake up in a bad state because of the bed or the morning itself; we wake up with a mindset that clouds our perception and shapes our attitude for the day. It's not the bed that's wrong—it's our thoughts, worries, or unresolved emotions that dictate how we approach the hours ahead. By recognizing that our mindset is the true source of negativity, we can take ownership of our perspective and make intentional choices to shift it.

A better morning, and ultimately a better day, starts not with the side of the bed we roll out of. Rather, think about it like this: *"You don't get up on the wrong side of the bed...you get up in the wrong side of your head."*

That said, we all have to expect there will be times when we are lost and make a few wrong choices. You may be there now. This is an okay place to be, just not an okay place to stay.

There are two powerful questions which sum up this principle of embracing the struggle. Let's call them the 2Qs, and here they are:

1) What am I seeing in my world (what's happening)?

2) What am I saying to myself about this?

You can all be a "self-coach" to support yourself in life. You can identify something in your life that needs to be different or better, and you can coach yourself to move to and create that place. The thing is, you must have a framework and a set of tools to use when needed.

H.U.T. and the 2Qs are such tools. Asking the first of the 2Qs creates a strong and focused awareness of your situation, and your answer to the second question creates your emotions and actions to move forward.

Your strength and growth are available in how you answer the second question. And trust me on this . . . it is a choice. I'll repeat it . . .it is a choice; it's YOUR choice.

Think about Nelson Mandela, for example. He endured unimaginable hardship during his 27 years in prison, facing brutality, ridicule, and humiliation from his captors. Despite this, he emerged not with bitterness, but with a profound commitment to forgiveness and reconciliation. Mandela believed that harboring anger would only prolong his own suffering, so he chose to see beyond the cruelty inflicted upon him and work toward a future of peace and unity for South Africa. He famously said, "As I walked out the door toward the gate that would lead to my freedom, I knew if I didn't leave my bitterness and hatred behind, I'd still be in prison." For Mandela, forgiveness was not merely an act of kindness but a necessary step to achieving true freedom—for himself and for his country.

In my list of personal heroes, Mandela is joined by Mel Fisher ("today's the day"), Welles Crowther (the man in the red bandana on 9/11), Mother Theresa, my young friend with cancer in Dick's Sporting Goods, my brother-in-law Bobby, and me after my accident . . .it all comes down to how you answer the second question.

If you get stuck, you'll likely resemble the comment made by an airline pilot when he came on the intercom and said: "Hello, ladies and gentlemen, this is your captain speaking. I have good news and bad news. The bad news is we're lost; the good news is we're making great time." Your answer to the second question gets you back on track and headed to your destination.

Turn to Your Spirit

Think about what you're saying to yourself about **all the areas** of your life right now. Are you good? Are you holding useful thoughts? Or do you need to work on your self-talk and inner dialogue? If you do, welcome to life—me too. We need to do the work.

I want you to imagine if someone showed up and took over your life. What would they change? What would they focus on to create a stronger and more focused "you?" How would they effectively leverage and gain value from the 2Qs above? What would they do to lead you to practice "H.U.T." more effectively? How could they get you to embrace your struggles? The good news is you don't need someone to show up to answer these questions . . . you are here, and you can do it yourself.

I want you to imagine if someone showed up and took over your life. What would they change?

Often, the voice between your ears is negative and filled with non-useful thoughts . . .the voice that comes from your Spirit is always helpful and encouraging and wants what's best for you. Your Spirit wants to support you in answering the second question of the 2Qs: *What am I saying to myself about this?*

You always have a choice as to which one you'll listen to and which you will ignore. Here's the thing, though: your brain's voice is usually louder. It can be heard amongst the world's noise and is often intertwined.

Ever been in the noise of social media, and you see someone's post who you see is "doing better" than you or so it seems, and your shitty voice starts ranting?

Your judgment of this person "doing better" than you is subjective. And . . .why do you care? If they're doing well . . ..great. Other people, whether IRL or online, are not a metric against which you can be measured. You measure yourself against how well you're living your truth, right? How well are you living your values . . .how significant is your growth?

In fact, let's not use the word "measure," because that implies you could give yourself a failing grade. How about evaluate? You should evaluate and observe yourself, celebrate the growth, take a deep breath, smile, and then take action to improve where you need to. It's just life. It's a beautiful and fragile experience we're all having, and you're in the driver's seat.

Be Still, Again

When I was fourteen, my mom told me to cut the grass. I did not want to and felt one of my brothers should do it. My mom and I argued (yes, I was just being a punk), and as I stood over the lawn mower about to start it, she put her head out the side door, glaring at me, and said, "You cut the grass." I glared back, pulled the cord to start that mower, and in the nasty noise of the mower, I replied with a short phrase that rhymes with "cut the grass." Yes, not one of my Hallmark moments, and one I am ashamed of to this day. My mom's face changed in an instant, and she covered the 10 yards to me faster than an NFL running back, shutting down the mower, banishing me to my room, and saying, "You just wait until —." You know the rest, " . . . until your father gets home." While I could not hear myself above the noise of the lawn mower, how many of you cannot hear yourself over the busy-ness and noise of the "lawn mower of life" you fire up each day?

While your brain's voice and the world's noise exist in your daily life, your Spirit resides in stillness. It loves hanging out when you meditate, pray, journal, take a slow walk on the beach, and employ many other practices of a powerful principle known as *being still*.

The ability to be still, to disconnect from the busy and crazy hustle we often call life, serves you well as you self-coach with the 2Qs.

Remember this? The Spirit wants only what's good for you. It wants you to create fulfillment, resilience, and growth for you and for those you love and those you lead.

Kobe Bryant was an American basketball star who died with his daughter, Gianna, and seven others when the helicopter they were in tragically crashed into a Los Angeles hillside due to foul weather and fog. I often watch his short clip on Jay Shetty's podcast when he says this about stillness, thoughts, and emotions.[6]

What I try to do is just try to be still. And understand that things come and go. Emotions come and go. The important thing is to accept them all. To embrace them all. And then you can choose to do with them what you want. Versus being controlled by emotion.

Think about stillness as often as you can, especially when you're in the struggles and shitshows and misfortunes of life. Call on the simple and powerful tools I've offered you.

Life has no pause button . . . it's always moving forward . . . are you?

My friends, always do the work to *embrace the struggle* when it arrives . . . it's the genuine path forward for you.

---

6 https://www.youtube.com/watch?v=U9hkls2HpZI

#6

ALWAYS ~~TRY~~ WORK TO BE BETTER

"No! Try not. Do. Or do not. There is no try."

—Yoda *(The Empire Strikes Back)*

Always ~~Try~~ Work to Be Better

What would the world be like if we, at birth, were given this instruction by our parents: "always work to be better?" (You probably noticed I changed the word "try" in the chapter title to "work." I'll tell you more about this later.) What if "working to be better" was ingrained in our brains like software that ran and produced a world of people who, each day, when they came back to life, had this as their primary focus? Always work to be better. How can you be better? What roles do you have in your life? Mom, dad, sister, brother, son, daughter, leader, friend, mentor, etc.? Do you live this philosophy of **arrfYl**? People who live with **arrfYl** are keenly aware of the vital need always to keep getting better.

As I talked about previously, my brother-in-law, Dr. Bobby "Doc" Sinnott, passed away from ALS a few years ago. It hurt like hell and still does. I've "embraced the struggle" of life without him and the hurt that lingers. His son, Matt, posted a video about Doc on YouTube called "Try to be better. Doc's Final Message" (see footnote[7]).

Doc and I spent much time together as he battled ALS, and I'm thankful for this gift of being together with him. The time with him made me a better man and more committed to continually working and improving. The reason I crossed out the word try

---

7 https://www.youtube.com/watch?v=o5ZGmQomxyg&t=64s

in the title of this chapter and replaced it with work is something Doc and I talked about . . .and laughed about.

Doc helped me write the chapter about his struggle in my book *Taking the Sh*t Out of the Show*. The book is seven short stories about people working to embrace their struggle and work to be better. Six of the seven stories are fiction; only Doc's is based on fact. The chapter title is simply *Bobby*. I would bring up my computer document on the big screen TV in his basement, and he'd scrunch up his nose when he didn't like my writing, and we'd work to get it more to his "voice." One day, he was consistently critical of my writing, and I stopped and asked him, "Who the **** are you all the sudden, Hemingway?" Man, did we have a great laugh then? I'll never forget that moment. A strong foundation for an **arrfYl** lifestyle is the commitment to improve and grow stronger.

When I ask people about their progress in an area of their lives, they often say, "I'm trying." Most times, this response and their energy have a defeated tone to it. They squint, purse their lips and/or tilt their head. They raise their shoulders in a move of uncertainty, or their shoulders merely drop. You see, I believe when you are "trying," there's an unconscious belief that you cannot do what you are focused on. Does this make sense to you?

I offer them the opportunity to consider that they are not trying but are doing the work. Some days, you do better; other days, perhaps not so good. You are doing the work.

How do you practice this? How do you actually "work to be better"? Well, it has much to do with what we've covered in this book.

I'll focus on four areas where I continue to do the work to get better: physical, mental, emotional, and spiritual.

I'll share some tools I use to stay on track and committed to growing in these areas.

Physical Work

I was once told the best way to work on getting better in terms of your health is to "eat less, move more." This resonated with me. Although I've never had a huge appetite, I like to eat, and for me, it's a lot about cheese and sandwiches. I live outside of Philadelphia, and the cheesesteaks are the best. I've grown to eat healthier . . . more salads, lean meats, and less carbs. This works for me, and something different may work for you.

There's a Japanese phrase, "*Hara hachi bu*," which translates to eat until you're 80% full. It is said to have originated in Okinawa to support people in creating healthy eating habits and maintaining a healthy weight. Someone once told me my stomach is about as big as my fist, and man, did this stay with me over the years as I contemplated the portion of food I would eat. Think about it. You should only eat enough food to fill a volume about 80% of your fist. Think about what you are saying to yourself about *what* you are eating and *how much* you are eating. Use your inner voice to establish and reinforce healthy eating habits.

I've also always enjoyed playing sports and working out with weights. In the summer, I run, paddleboard, surf, and walk to places if possible.

Break Up With Bad Habits

All of you probably remember a high school break-up with your first love. It's when you decide you no longer want to be committed to that person.

Why not apply that same idea to our bad habits? I often ask myself, "Where do I need a break-up?" This question gets me thinking about what I need to remove from my life. Sometimes, it's about spending less or no time with a person or group. Other times, it's about removing or limiting what I eat or drink. Sometimes it's about removing some inputs such as TV and social media from my life. I've included it here in terms of your physical health.

I enjoyed drinking vodka on the rocks with stuffed blue cheese olives. I enjoyed this way too much for many years for the wrong reasons. I guess "enjoy" is not the best choice of words for me. It was a way to fight my demons, or so I thought. It actually strengthened them. I struggled with alcohol for years and made many poor choices, most when I was drunk. I still drink, although mostly some red wine and beer, and nowhere near the quantities I used to consume. Trust me, this is a good thing for me and those I love.

One moment of realization was years ago when I was so drunk I could not ride a beach cruiser a mile back to our home. A beach cruiser is a bike with no gears, and simple brakes where all you need to do is gently push the pedals backwards. It has fat tires. I was riding on a flat road . . .and I could not ride a mile. I fell often, only to have my patient and loving brother-in-law, Danny—yes, there are two Dannys in my family—pick me up.

One particular fall was into a bunch of bushes where one of my flip-flops fell off. It was dark, and I was determined to find it. Danny stayed with me, and I finally resigned to his sound advice of returning in the morning. As I did, I removed my other flip-flop and tossed it into the bushes.

Danny laughed, shook his head and asked, "What are you doing?" I smiled and slurred, "Well, if anyone finds the first one, I want them to have both because these are a nice pair." Even in a drunken stupor, I suppose I still led with love to a degree.

Eating, drinking, and exercising are different for each of you. I broke up with vodka on the rocks with stuffed blue cheese olives. My question for you is this, "Who or what do you need to break up with to get better physically?"

Get Your Daily D.O.S.E.

Every brain releases neurotransmitters or chemicals. The four I've become fond of are what I call the "daily D.O.S.E.," which stands for **d**opamine, **o**xytocin, **s**erotonin, and **e**ndorphins.

Daily D.O.S.E.

dopamine
oxytocin
serotonin
endorphins

The table below explains the benefits of these four chemicals and how to trigger their release. Begin to do more of the activities to release them and see how this supports you doing the work to be better physically.

WHAT?	WHY?	HOW?
Dopamine	• inspiration • action • progress to goals and vision	• be organized • work at action level • celebrate • learn & discover • be BOLD with your vision • anticipate good things and accomplishments
Oxytocin *"cuddle drug"*	• intimacy • trust • connection • strong relationships	• hug • gift-giving • some foods:, eggs , bananas, pepper • deep breathing/ meditation • call or video/Facetime vs. text or email • eye-contact and attentiveness
Serotonin	• feelings of significance and self-esteem • good mood	• reflect on past achievements • practice gratitude • get outside in the sun (vitamin D) • read your vision • get a massage
Endorphins *"second wind"* *"runners high"*	• alleviate stress pain, anxiety, depressions	• exercise • laughter • scents (vanilla, lavender) • dark chocolate • spicy food • ginseng • listen to music & dance

Mental Work

To get better with your mental side, you must commit to awareness. You must do the work to monitor your thoughts and self-talk. In Navy SEAL training, the SEALs learn about what they call the **Big 4 of mental toughness**:

1) **Get control of your breathing.** I do breathing exercises for a few minutes each day. If you do, you know the benefit. If you don't, I recommend you surf the internet for beginner breathing exercises and get started. One simple breathing exercise is to breathe in for 4 seconds, hold your breath for 4 seconds, then breathe out for 4 seconds. Try this for 10 cycles.

2) **Get control over your self-talk, mental chatter, and negative mindset**. Remember, your life is lived between your ears; the SEALs know this in life-and-death situations. Your mind will quit before your body based on what you are saying to yourself. Sometimes you need to listen less to your negative and habitual chatter and talk more new, positive chatter.

Your brain will quit before your body.

---

3) **Use the right imagery and visualization to empower your emotions.** Do you visualize your day before you get out of bed? Do you visualize your workouts, meals, meetings, and difficult actions and conversations? I've come to understand if the SEALs do, it's probably a good idea for us as well. The

more you imagine something in your mind, the more it is likely to happen in reality.

4) Get task-focused on the next action.

As an example of how I put the Big 4 into practice, I knew that I am especially challenged by the second item—which is to get control over my self-talk, mental chatter, and negative mindset. To get control of that, I took up journaling. This helps increase my awareness of my self-talk and thoughts and reinforces the tremendous truth: *I am not my thoughts; I am the thinker of them*. Boom! When I get this, I realize I can sit with the negative ones, discard them, replace them, and practice H.U.T. (hold useful thoughts).

Emotional Work

I have always enjoyed learning about emotions and the field of psychology. I've come to understand that emotions drive our actions, which ultimately produce our outcomes. Some of these are the desired outcomes you seek, and others are not.

There is a great deal of research on human emotions. I work to stay aware of my emotional state and have a strategy to move out of the ones that don't serve me at the moment. The research I did on our emotions led to many theories, some very comprehensive and detailed. There is a simple—yet powerful one for me— that believes there are four primary emotions: Mad, sad, glad, and afraid. The simplicity of this helps me stay aware of my emotions because I can quickly assess where I am.

There is nothing wrong or negative about having any of these. What is essential if you want always to work to be better is to know that your emotional state is the force that causes you to take action. So, when you are mad (angry), you may say something hurtful that you'll later regret *or* you can take a walk or go to the gym for an intense workout. When you're glad about achievement, you could celebrate and perhaps have the infamous "one to many" drinks, **or** you could have a calm dinner with your significant other or a few friends or grab your journal and write some thoughts of gratitude. When you're sad, you could shut people out and not let them love you fiercely and perhaps become more miserable, **or** you could embrace your sadness and possibly seek some support to move you through it. When you're sad, you could remain in the noise of society and continue staying sad and not facing your sadness, **or** you could retreat to a place of solitude and sit with your sadness, embrace this emotion and then begin to see the other side and move through your sadness back toward joy. You always have a choice, right?

When you're afraid about your future, and uncertainty is present, you can create more stress and anxiety by contemplating all the negative things that could happen, **or** you could think about your vision of how you want things to be and take action to move toward that. I never have anxiety about my past. My anxiety comes from thinking about the past and mistakes and bad things that happened, and then bringing the possibility of them happening again into my present moment. It is remembering the past that brings anxiety about my uncertainty about the future. This reminds me of a few lines from the song Dustland Fairytale sung by The Killers:

"And the decades disappear like sinking ships but we persevere. God gives us hope, but we still fear what we don't know. The mind is poison."

And you know what? Most of what you and I fear and get anxious about never happens. Yes, the mind can be poison. When I'm scared, I first call on the Spirit to support me (remember Chapter 1?). I ask the Spirit to fill me with a calm and trusting mind.

Spiritual Work

How do you nourish your Spirit? How do you grow in this area? I'll offer you a few ways which work for me.

I attend mass regularly on Sunday and a few times during the week. If you are not a member of a church or have gotten away from going, maybe now is the time to reengage, return to your church, or find a new one. If your "church" is not a physical structure—maybe it's out in nature—and it supports you connecting with your Spirit, right on!

One of the best ways I can nourish my Spirit is to be with someone who has a solid connection to their Spirit. Think about Mother Theresa, Welles Crowther, Nelson Mandela, my brother-in-law Bobby, and others I've mentioned earlier in this book. I believe the Spirit is an energy in each of us, and it is good when it is connected between two or more people.

And you know one of the best people for me to be with? A baby? Yes, a baby. Their connection to the Spirit is intensely strong when they arrive in this world. So was yours when you were born.

It has to be because your Spirit, your 4th energy, ultimately keeps your body working. Your heart and brain and lungs contribute to your body working, and I've come to understand your Spirit is the true source of life. When I died, my heart didn't leave my body, nor my brain or lungs. What I experienced was my Spirit leaving. I'm sure you've experienced the joy of holding a newborn, looking into their eyes, and perhaps having your finger in their tiny hand as they squeeze. It does not matter if they smile, fart, poop their diaper or vomit . . . it's a slice of Heaven as far as I'm concerned.

As I write this, we've been blessed with a great-nephew and great-niece (Bobby and Trish's grandchildren), and being with them is perfect for my connection with Spirit. You probably feel the energy shift when a baby appears at your work, school, or another event. They become the center of attention because their energy fills us, and the world has not yet gone to work to affect and diminish their connection with their Spirit.

Another way that works for me to "feed my Spirit," as my friend Cate Heamen, CEO of Prelude Solutions, describes this, is to focus on my "35." Let me explain.

What do you believe are the most important 35 minutes of your week? I believe it's the first five minutes each morning when I "come back to life" and transition from sleep to my day. I have an acronym (no surprise here, I bet) that I go through when I awake.

My current "35" is what I call SVMA. For 5 minutes at the start of every day, I think about each part of SVMA:

"S" stands for Spirit. I take the time to pray, breathe, realize, and "feel" the Spirit within me, the Spirit that is a part of me.

"V" stands for vision. This is the story of my year and the things I want to achieve and accomplish in the critical areas of my life: Faith, relationships, health, business, Finance, fun, creativity, etc. I reflect on where I am for the year and what still requires focus.

"M" stands for mindset. I monitor my thoughts and self-talk, removing the negative and replacing it with positive and useful thoughts to create my emotions and guide my actions. H.U.T.: Hold useful thoughts.

"A" is for action. I think of three, four, or five actions I must take today to drive my vision. I work with any fear or procrastination that may be present to overcome it and commit to the action.

This exercise is well-received in my workshops when the participants create their "35." I've received feedback similar to the excerpt below from an email I received.

"Through your work, I have fully embraced the first five minutes of the day, and that is truly the difference maker in allowing me to work through these different parts of myself while still showing up and serving the day."

Here are a few "35" from others:

GATE - Gratitude, Attitude, Talk, Energy

LEAD - Love, Evolve, Action, Divine

F3 - Faith, Family, Freedom

FORT - Faith, Optimism, Resilience, Thankfulness

GOAT - Gratitude, Optimistic, Action, Trust

GEM - Gratitude, Enjoyment, Mindset

This concept of the "35" results from a morning when I woke in a disturbed and negative frame of mind. My wife, Lisa, and I had been arguing about something I realized was somewhat ridiculous, and one of my speaking gigs had been canceled.

This was about two months before my brother-in-law Bobby passed. That particular morning, I thought about how, when we put him to bed at night, Bobby would lie flat and have us hold his ankles and push with his legs until his head touched the headboard. He wanted to be up in the hospital bed so that when we raised it, he would sit straighter, and his breathing would be easier.

As I thought of Bobby and his courage and Faith in his struggle and how he lived with **arrfYl**, I pushed back until my head touched the headboard . . . and you know what? My perspective shifted. In a second, my victim mentality was gone; I smiled and got out of bed, focused on creating a good day, and got back to living with **arrfYl**. I apologized, told Lisa I loved her and focused on my business to drive more relationships and keynotes. It was a great day. Regardless of where I am, I have touched the headboard every morning for over two years and will continue until I die again. Maybe give it a try.

Be the Goat

"In short, the straightforward and good person should be like a smelly goat—you know when they are in the room with you."
—Marcus Aurelius

I love this quote from Marcus Aurelius, a Roman emperor from the second century. I first came across it on October 11, 2023. I know the exact date because I was reading and posting a quote each day that year from the daily Stoic calendar. It goes well with my philosophy of **arrfY1**. I know you're probably thinking, "What does a smelly goat have to do with living a radically reverent life?" Let me explain.

Marcus is talking about knowing what someone is about when they show up—their good traits should be as unavoidable as the smell of a goat.

I think the same should be true of a person living with **arrfY1**. You should know they are in the room because of *how* they are. They will bring a specific energy of curiosity and authenticity, a way of being, to any room they enter. Most importantly, you "know them" because they're committed to doing the work to continue getting better, growing, and creating fulfillment and resilience . . . and they bring love.

A better quote for this chapter might be this one from Charles Bukowski, author of *Tales of Ordinary Madness* (although I love the smelly goat quote and had to go with that one).

*"The free soul is rare, but you know it when you see it—
basically because you feel good, very good, when you are near
or with them."*

I researched the definition of a free soul (surprised?). I came across one from quora.com: "A free soul is a person who has reached a certain degree of maturity and emotional stability, based on confidence and independence."

Whether you're called a smelly goat by Marcus or a free soul by Charles, when you are committed to always doing the work to be better, you are living with **arrfYl**. Are you one of these "people?

A free soul is a person who has reached a certain degree of maturity and emotional stability, based on confidence and independence.

To live with **arrfYl** is always to work to be better, and when you do, you'll naturally evolve to support others on their journey to be better as well. The Spiritual teacher, Ram Dass, offered us a brief statement to reflect on, which, when internalized, is powerful beyond measure. Ram said, "We're all just walking one another home." Wow, right? And so freakin' true.

Think about that quote. *Walking* is movement, meaning you are still on the journey. *Home* for me means a destination, a place your walking will take you. For me, this place is the same place I experienced when I died. It is a place of peace, joy, and love . . .many call it Heaven and trust me, these words we're familiar with in this life don't come close to describing the next one. So, you have this to look forward to . . .if you choose.

Always work to be better and live the insight offered by St. Francis DeSales when he said, "Be who you are and be that well." Always work to be better.

#7

CONTEMPLATE YOUR MORTALITY

"We have two lives, and the second one begins when we realize we only have one."

—Confucius

Contemplate Your Mortality

As we come to a close with this book, perhaps I stirred your Soul, challenged your thinking, or even planted some seeds of impact, influence, and inspiration for you to live with **arrfY1**. And now you may be thinking, "Wow, Danny, I'm really impressed with the title of this chapter. Great way to end your book, having me think about my own death."

I get it. Stay with me. The quote above is a favorite of mine; Confucius got me thinking about that second life he refers to. And I came to realize that, in my view, the "second one" begins each day we rouse from our sleep and come back to life.

The mindset of contemplating your mortality, of being aware of the fact you will not live forever, is one I've begun to explore much more over the past five years or so. I've lost too many friends to cancer, heart attacks, and ALS. I recently turned sixty years old and have watched the world continue to turn. Having already died once for a brief period, you'd think I would have "gotten" this concept of contemplating my mortality as a away to force me to focus on life . . . sooner.

But no, it took me a few years. During my keynote speech, I usually remind my audience—like I did with you in the preface of this book—that they will take about 23,000 breaths today, and their hearts will beat about 100,000 times. That's over thirty-six and a half million heartbeats in the next year.

And while these bodily functions are automatic, they're not guaranteed. This simple yet profound realization can help you develop a genuine and consistent reverence for YOUR life.

Reflecting on my mortality in this way has transformed my life and I know it can do the same for you.

Marcus Aurelius (he of the "smelly goat"), known as the last good emperor of Rome, wrote extensively about mortality and was consistent in contemplating it. Two of my favorite Marcus quotes are below.

> *"When you arise in the morning, think of what a precious privilege it is to be alive—to breathe, to think, to enjoy, to love . . ."*

~~

> *"You could leave life right now. Let that determine what you do and say and think."*

What do you think of these quotes? Do you see how Marcus's contemplation of his mortality during a few moments in the morning, the awareness of what he will do and say and think, is one of resilience, gratitude, and positivity? Do you see how this morning ritual led to this mindset being the foundation for his life? Do you have this? Could you begin to choose this way of thinking more often? Would you? When?

The contemplation of my mortality is not a detailed movie I play in my mind. I don't sit and wonder about when and how I am going to die. Instead, I smile and think, "Yep, Danny boy, you ain't gonna be here forever." And from that reminder to myself, I can get focused on the gift of life and be fully alive and engaged and focused on the areas of my life where I want to make a difference.

Contemplating your mortality should not stress you out or produce anxiety about how much time you have left. Instead, it should produce joy, gratitude, kindness, self-love, forgiveness, focus, and many more beautiful energies.

When you contemplate your mortality, you are in the future—think about it . . . you will not draw your last breath in the past! And hopefully, contemplating your mortality should keep you out of the pain of your past. Too many people live in regret and create the negative energy of playing things over and over in their minds. They wish they had done something differently or things were different.

Too many people live in regret and create the negative energy of playing things over and over in their minds.

Trust me, once gain. I have thought a million times about lowering that ladder so many years ago and how I should have stopped and considered another route. But you know what? All those hours of thinking about the past brought me nothing but more pain, suffering, and vodka . . . and no forward movement.

I did not think July 28, 1992, would be my last day alive, and it was . . . then it wasn't. After the accident, I did think about the day of the accident and the experience of dying. I thought about it over and over and over. This changed when I walked into . . .

and, more importantly, out of a phone booth in the Outer Banks of North Carolina.

I was dangerously close to taking my life and had looked to buy a hose to put one end in the tailpipe of my Jeep and the other in the driver's window and leave the engine running. I did not buy the hose that day because I believe one of my Angels showed up. She was about five feet tall, eighty years old, with suntan wrinkled skin and a bright white smile sitting beneath piercing—and I mean piercing—blue eyes. She said something to me; to this day, I don't remember what. I remember she interrupted my thinking.

Instead of the hose, I went and got drunk, then stopped in the phone booth on my way back to my motel. After a brief call to my mom, I walked out of the booth, and the voice of my Spirit whispered, "I wonder what it's going to be like when I get better." This was the moment things shifted for me, the moment I began to understand and explore living with **arrfYl**.

Now, some 30+ years later, the **arrfYl** mindset becomes more vital to me daily. It's also reassuring that I used "wonder" when my Spirit spoke, a keyword associated with the definition of the word "reverence" in **arrfYl**. Reverence is to hold a wonder and an awe about your life journey. When I left the phone booth, something shifted; I focused on being alive. Thinking about the fact that I will not be here forever was not a depressing, sad & morbid thought. Instead . . . it has become one of inspiration and empowerment.

I began to think of what I heard from a priest once when he said, "I have had the great privilege of offering Mass several times in the many convents of the Missionaries of Charity sisters. So, I am used to seeing these words in a prominent place in the sacristy where priests prepare for Holy Mass:

Priest of Jesus Christ, celebrate this Holy Mass as if it were your first Mass, your last Mass, your only Mass.

When I heard this, I converted this statement to just being Danny Bader and being given another day alive.

Danny, celebrate today as if it were your first day, your last day, your only day."

What if you and me and all of us do this:

Live today as if it's your first day, your last day, your only day. Do this over and over and over again . . . and then it will all be okay.

And when I draw my last breath again, and if I'm aware of life ending, I'm going to do my best to be wearing a smile. I wish the same for you.

Epilogue

I hope you saw how these seven principles I write and speak about—and offer you in this book—overlap. No powerful personal growth principle stands alone. They need one another. It's an approach, a collection of principles that will help you create a path to more fulfillment and resilience in your life.

Now it's your turn to apply them to your own life. What do you do *now* when you get stuck? What could you do differently to change, grow, get unstuck, whatever you call it.

It's freakin' simple: your approach—the principles you
practice—create your life.

Every day, your thoughts and actions demonstrate your choices about how you want to live your life. I've found the principles in this book drive my own achievement, success, fulfillment, contentment, and my resilience . . . my ability to move through the shitshows. Period! They can do the same for you.

Don't focus on changing your life. Instead, focus on strengthening your approach to being fully alive, to being radical in how you express your reverence for all aspects of your life. Enjoy the journey.

About the Author

Danny Bader is a respected author and popular keynote speaker whose near-death experience has shaped his unique life philosophy. Known for best-selling books like *Back to Life*, *I Met Jesus for a Miller Lite*, *Abraham's Diner*, and *Taking the Sh*t Out of the Show*, Danny goes beyond typical motivational speaking to inspire deep and lasting personal growth.

His concept of the "4th energy"—a profound spiritual foundation—is central to his teachings on resilience and fulfillment. Through his journey and roles as a husband, father, son and friend, Danny helps audiences connect with their Spirit, fostering resilience, joy, and purpose that positively impact personal and professional lives.

Danny splits his time between Conshohocken, PA, and Cape May, NJ.

Made in the USA
Middletown, DE
23 March 2025

73092308R00066